wild Animals in the Park

Verse by Ginny McIntyre
Illustrations by Jean and Lance Rudegeair

Copyright © 1991 Antioch Publishing Company
ISBN 0-89954-398-7
Made in the United States of America

 Antioch Publishing Company
Yellow Springs, Ohio 45387

White-Tailed Deer

I am a deer
With a white tail to wag;
If you see me running,
You'll think it's a flag.

With my long, graceful legs,
I can leap very high—
You'll see just how fast
When I pass you by!

My little fawn babies
Aren't easily found;
In coats brown and speckly,
They blend with the ground.

Raccoon

They call me a bandit
Because of my mask,
And prowling for food
At night is my task.

All through the nighttime
I swim, climb, and run.
I like to go fishing
For food and for fun.

When you see me walking,
You'll say, "There he goes,
The night's furry bandit
On his tippy toes."

Black Bear

I am a black bear
And you may find me
Scratching my back
Against a tall tree.

All through the summer,
I eat berries and fruits,
Digging into the ground
And eating tree roots.

When you see me strolling,
You'll think I am slow,
But when I want to run—
Just watch me go!

Porcupine

I am a porcupine.
I'm not very shy.
I snort and I bark,
I squeal and I cry.

It's not that I'm angry;
It's just how I talk.
My coat's made of needles
That shake when I walk.

Twigs, leaves, and tree bark
Are what I like to eat,
But salt is a special
And favorite treat.

Red Fox

I am a fox.
I'm shy and I'm quick.
When I disappear,
You'll think it's a trick.

I hunt for my food.
I'm rarely alone.
In fields or in woods,
I make my home.

Our babies are "kits"
And with them we share;
Both I and my mate
Give them love and good care.

Rabbit

I am a rabbit.
My back legs are long,
So I can move quickly
If anything's wrong.

My long, furry ears
Hear any small sound,
And if I'm frightened,
I run underground.

I look for green grasses
When I want to eat,
But green leaves and veggies
Are my favorite treats.

Opossum

I am a 'possum.
You just may find me
Asleep in the hollow
Of a tall, shady tree.

But if you should scare me,
As it's often said,
I will "play 'possum"
And pretend that I'm dead.

But when you have gone,
And I am alone,
I'll wake up again,
And find my way home!

<u>Skunk</u>

I am a striped skunk
With black, fluffy fur.
The noise that I make
Sounds like a "churr."

I'm easily known
By my long stripe of white.
I waddle, eat insects,
And sleep through the night.

We dance in a circle,
For skunks like to play,
But if we lift our tails high,
It means "Stay away!"

Squirrel

I am a squirrel.
You'll see I am bold,
And when I am angry,
I splutter and scold.

By my big, bushy tail
You'll recognize me.
I live in a twig nest
Atop an old tree.

I like to store nuts
While the weather's still warm,
Then I stay in my nest
Through the cold winter storms.

Beaver

I am a beaver.
You'll see me near lakes
Or near the lodges
My mate and I make.

With my big, sharp front teeth,
I cut down the logs,
And dam up the rivers
To make lakes and bogs.

When I walk, I waddle;
I'm not very trim.
My tail's like a paddle,
So I like to swim.

Bobcat

I am a bobcat
With a short, stubby tail.
At night I will wander
Alone on a trail.

I'm usually found
In a rough, rocky place.
I have spots on my coat
And a beard on my face.

When I am a baby,
My fur's bright and bold;
My colors will fade, though,
As I become old.

Wild Animals in the Park

Animals in the park or any outdoor area may seem friendly or cuddly, but they are wild creatures. They are happiest when left alone by humans.

Try to watch the animals from a distance. If you are close enough that they have to change how they are acting, you are too close.

The best way to help the animals is to keep their park or living area (called a habitat) clean, so please don't litter. Animals can be hurt by broken glass or trapped in plastic containers.